PAPER WORLD

STYLISH PAPER MODELS
TO POP-OUT AND CREATE

HELEN FRIEL

LOM
ART

Models and illustrations
by Helen Friel

Edited by Jocelyn Norbury
Cover Design by Angie Allison
Designed by Mina Bach
Photography by Jasper Fry

First published in Great Britain in 2018 by LOM ART,
an imprint of Michael O'Mara Books Limited,
9 Lion Yard, Tremadoc Road, London SW4 7NQ

W www.mombooks.com

F Michael O'Mara Books

Y @OMaraBooks

A CIP catalogue record for this book is available from the British Library.

ISBN: 978-1-910552-70-4

2 4 6 8 10 9 7 5 3 1

This book was printed in China

CONTENTS

Model 1

TROPICAL
TOUCAN

Model 2

VINTAGE
CAMERA

Model 3

FISH OUT
OF WATER

Model 4

AMAZING
ARMADILLO

Model 5

STYLISH
SUCCULENT

Model 6

BIG APPLE
DOUGHNUT

Model 7

FRUITY
FIESTA

Model 8

BUTTERFLY
COLLECTOR

Model 9

PARTY
PIÑATA

Model 10

SNAPPY
FISH

PLUS
STYLISH PAPER
SETS TO CREATE

A PASSION FOR PAPER ...

This collection of models began with my affinity for unusual animals. I originally made the armadillo and piranha for my own house, and they inspired me to go on to create the range that you see in this book.

"THE AIM IS TO SHARE MY PASSION FOR THE WONDERS OF PAPER."

The models have been devised by the same development process that I use for professional media projects. However, they are also designed to be made by everyone, whatever their level of skill. The aim is to share my passion for the wonders of paper, and to enable people to create some beautiful models for their own homes.

PAPER AS ART

As a paper engineer, I love the idea that paper doesn't have to be one-dimensional, flimsy and throwaway. I hope that the models in this book show just how versatile it can be.

CREATE A PAPER WORLD

Anyone can put these models together, from complete beginners onwards — it's the paper-modelling equivalent of painting by numbers. All of the pieces are pre-cut and creased, but you will also need a clear, all-purpose glue and a toothpick, or anything else pointy, like a pencil. The toothpick helps with any corners that are a bit fiddly, and can also be used to apply glue to small areas. Instructions and some notes are provided with each project. If you follow the numbering system you can't go wrong.

There are some hints on the next page to get you started.

"PAPER DOESN'T HAVE TO BE ONE-DIMENSIONAL, FLIMSY AND THROWAWAY."

Helen

HINTS

- The general rule is to start gluing at tab 1 and simply follow the numbers in order.

- The numbers in white circles indicate the points at which you apply the glue. The corresponding point has the same number without a circle.

- Apply glue to the whole of the numbered tab, not just to the white circle. Use as little glue as possible to keep your models neat. You can always add more if necessary.

- Make sure your glue is NOT water-based (such as PVA). Water-based glues can cause the paper to wrinkle.

- To glue accurately you can use a toothpick to apply or choose a glue with a precision applicator.

- Make sure each tab is dry before you move onto the next, especially on curved edges. This will give you a neater finish.

- The numbers are a guide for the easiest way to complete the model but everyone works differently, so if you're finding something difficult try it in a different order.

Tropical Toucan

CREATE THIS TROPICAL TOUCAN

Transport yourself to a lush green wonderland with this tropical toucan. And here's a fun feathered fact — toucans are known for their large, colourful bills. At around 20 centimetres long, they have the largest bill in relation to body size of any bird in the world, so use plenty of glue to fix the beak on to your beautiful bird.

1. Press out parts A to E.

2. Glue parts A and B together using tabs 1 to 7.

3. Glue part C to part B using tabs 8 to 14.

4. Glue part D to part B using tab 15.

5. Glue part D to part ABC using tabs 16 to 21.

6. Glue part E together using tab 22.

7. Glue part E to part B using tabs 23. To attach the beak apply a generous amount of glue to part B and hold in place until the glue is completely dry.

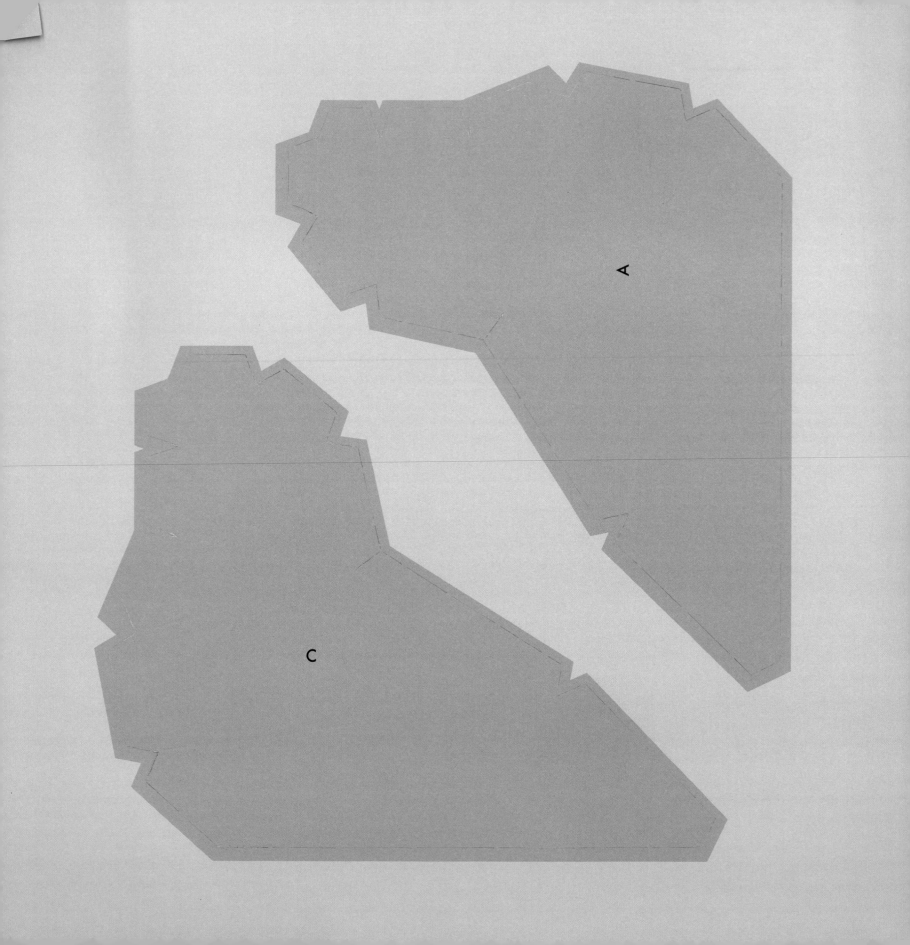

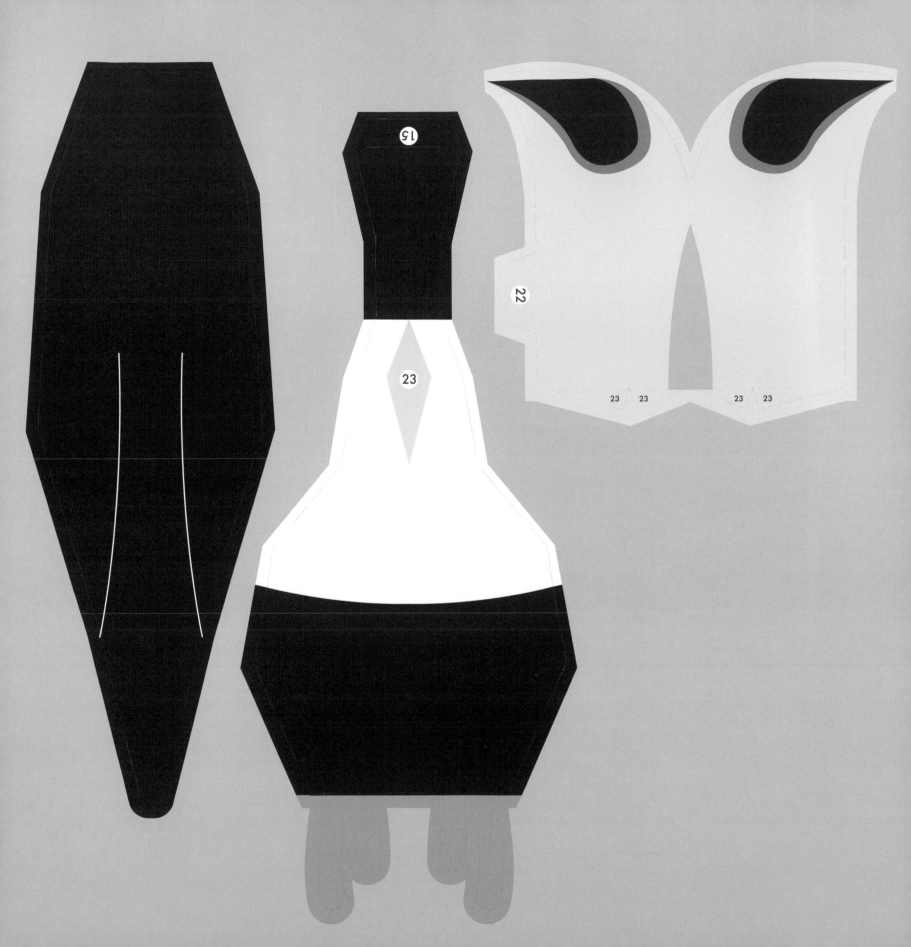

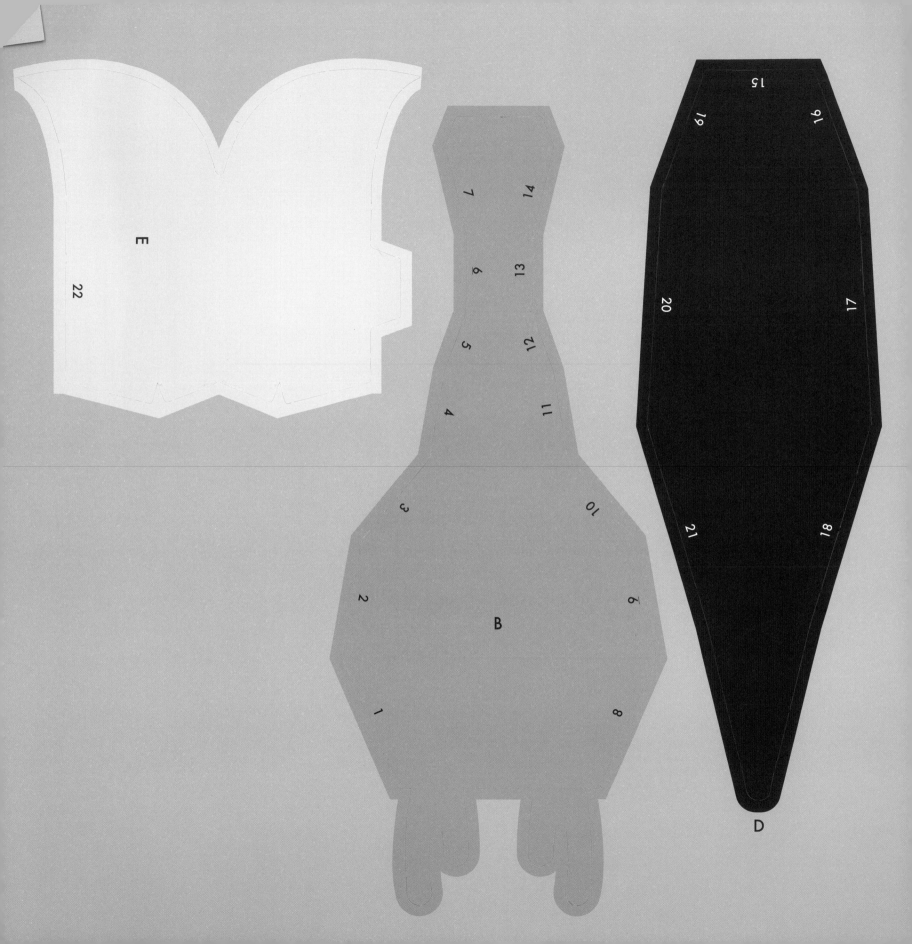

GET SNAP-HAPPY

Did you know that in the early days of photography it could take several minutes to capture an image because exposure times were so long? That's why nobody cracks a smile in those nineteenth century photographs.

1. Press out parts A to D.

2. Glue part A together using tabs 1 to 4.

3. Glue part B to part A using tabs 5 to 9.

4. Glue the flap of part A to AB using tabs 10.

5. Glue part C together using tab 11.

6. Glue part C to part A using tabs 12.

7. Glue part D to part C using tabs 13.

35mm

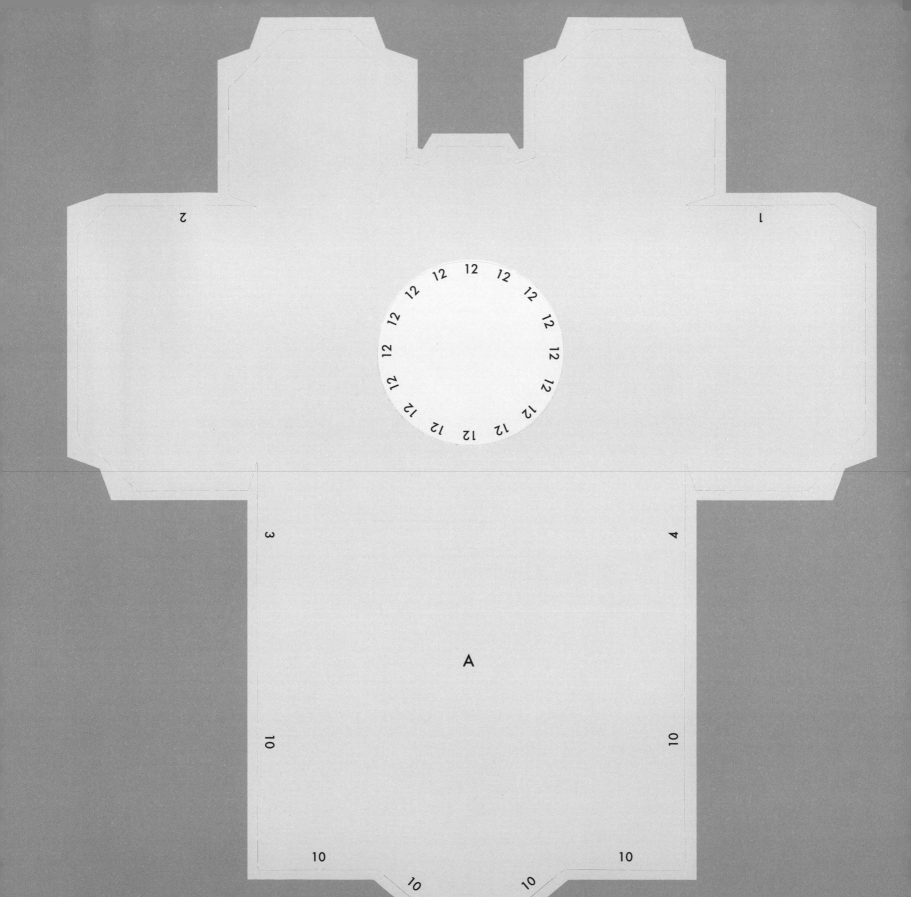

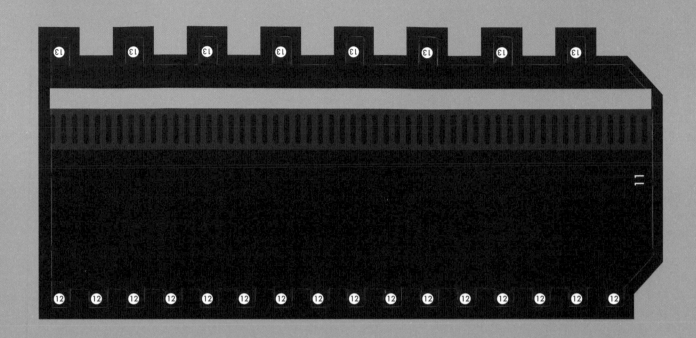

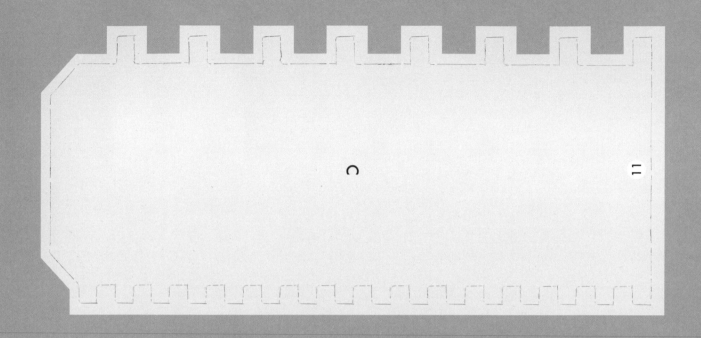

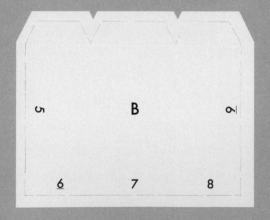

Fish out of Water

NOTHING FISHY HERE...

... But some goldfish have been known to grow to up to half a metre long. However, they're known to adapt to the size of their habitat, so you should have no problem with this little one. Maybe don't let it near any actual water.

1. Press out parts A to E.

2. Glue part A together using tabs 1 to 15.

3. Glue part B to part A using tabs 16. Use the lighter grey marks on part A and part B to make sure the pieces are correctly aligned.

4. Attach part C through part AB and secure on the bottom using tab 17.

5. Attach part D through part AB in the same way and slot on to part C using tabs 18 and 19. You may need to adjust parts C and D when they are glued to make sure they are upright.

6. Attach part E to part D using tab 20. Once everything is dry, gently bend the fish and seaweed to give a realistic 'wavy' look.

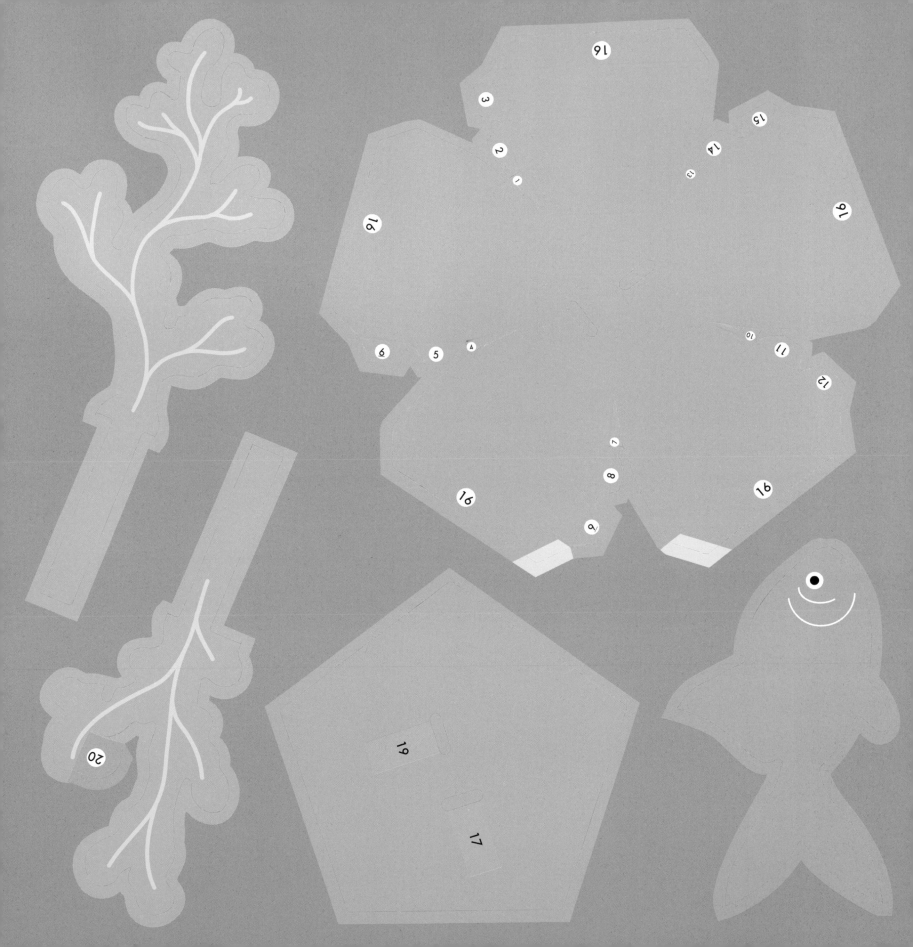

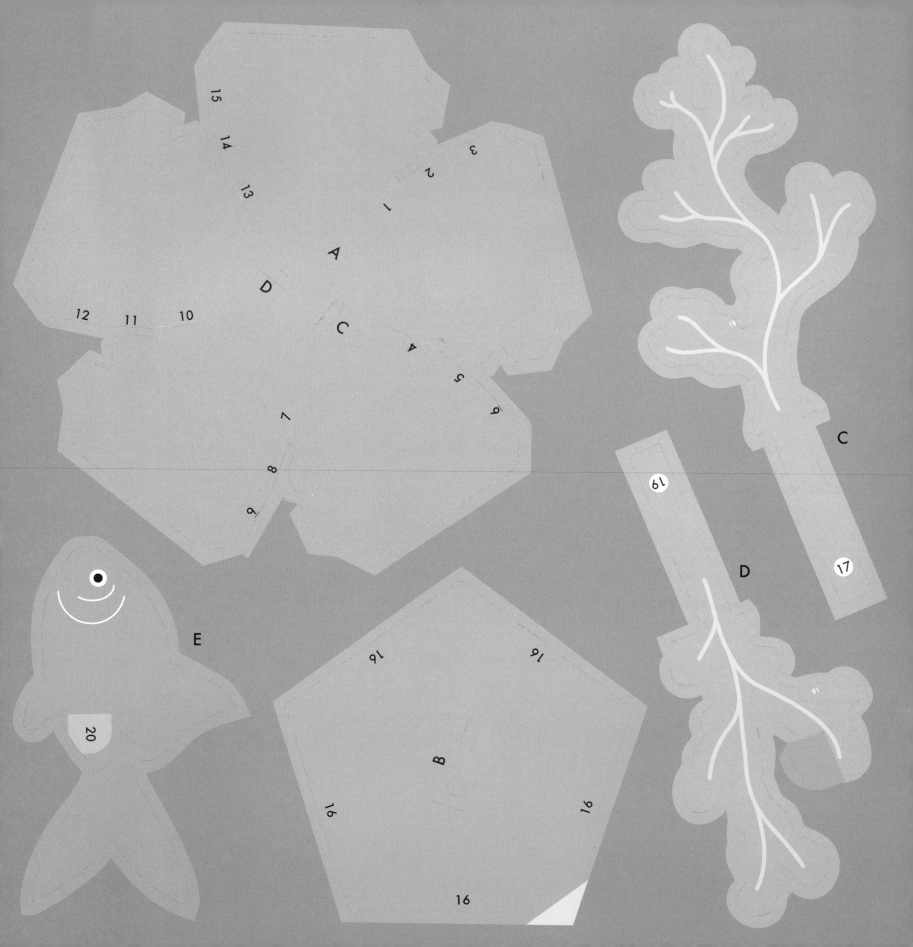

Amazing Armadillo

MAKE THIS COLOURFUL ARMADILLO

This cool creature is having a totally tropical time poolside. But did you know that the name armadillo comes from the Spanish for 'little armoured one'? Pretty sure you can call this guy anything you like.

1. Press out parts A to N.

2. Glue part A together using tabs 1 to 12.

3. Glue part B together using tabs 13 to 27.

4. Glue part B to part C using tabs 28 and 29.

5. Glue part D to part C using tabs 30 and 31.

6. Glue part E to part C using tabs 32 and 33.

7. Glue part F to part C using tabs 34 and 35.

8. Glue part A to part C using tabs 36 to 39.

9. Glue part G together using tabs 40 to 43.

10. Glue part G to part A using tabs 44 and 45.

11. Glue part H together using tabs 46 to 51.

12. Glue part H to part B using tab 52.

13. Glue part I together using tabs 53 and 54. Use something pointy, like a toothpick or pencil, to hold the tab inside the feet until the glue is completely dry.

14. Glue part J together using tabs 55 and 56.

15. Glue part K together using tabs 57 and 58.

16. Glue part L together using tabs 59 and 60.

17. Glue parts I to L to part C using tabs 61 to 64.

18. Glue part M to part G using tabs 65 and 66.

19. Take both parts N and fold. Push through the slots on the head and position as you like.

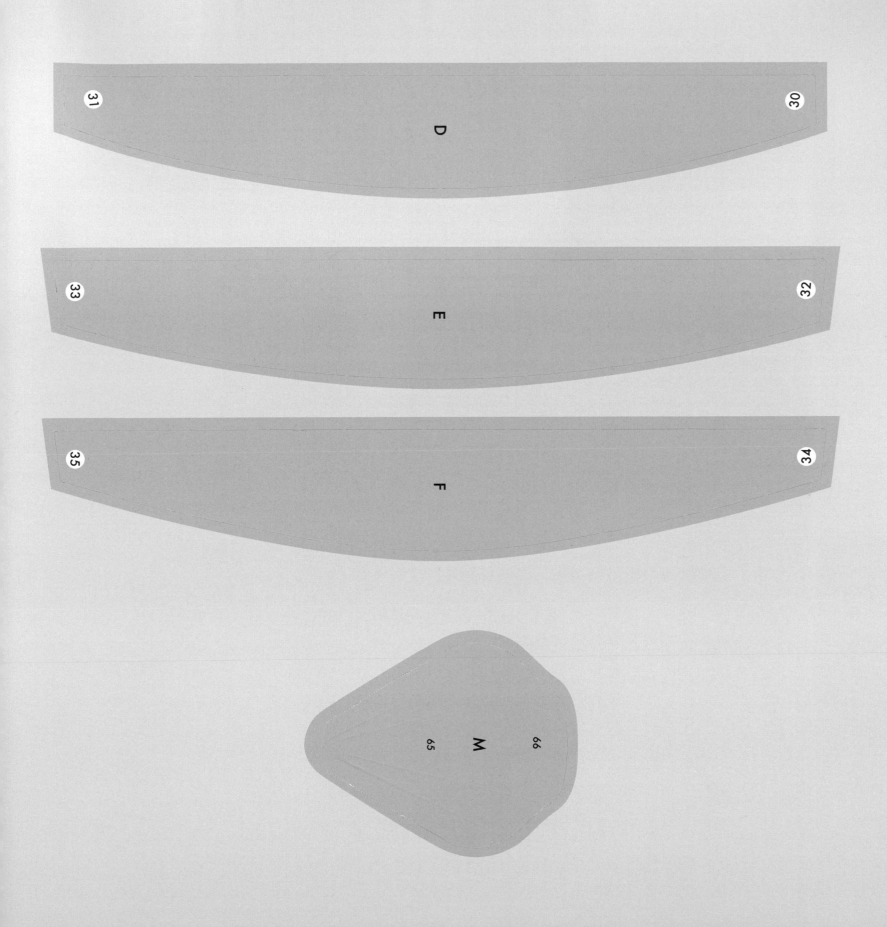

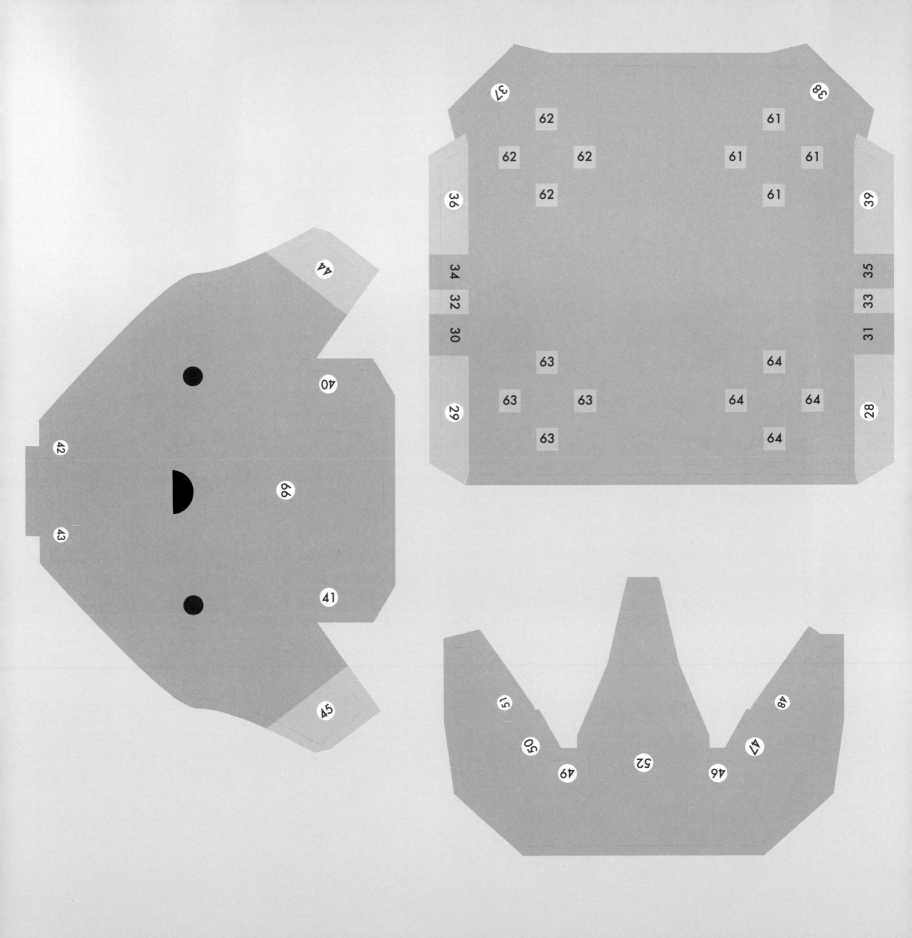

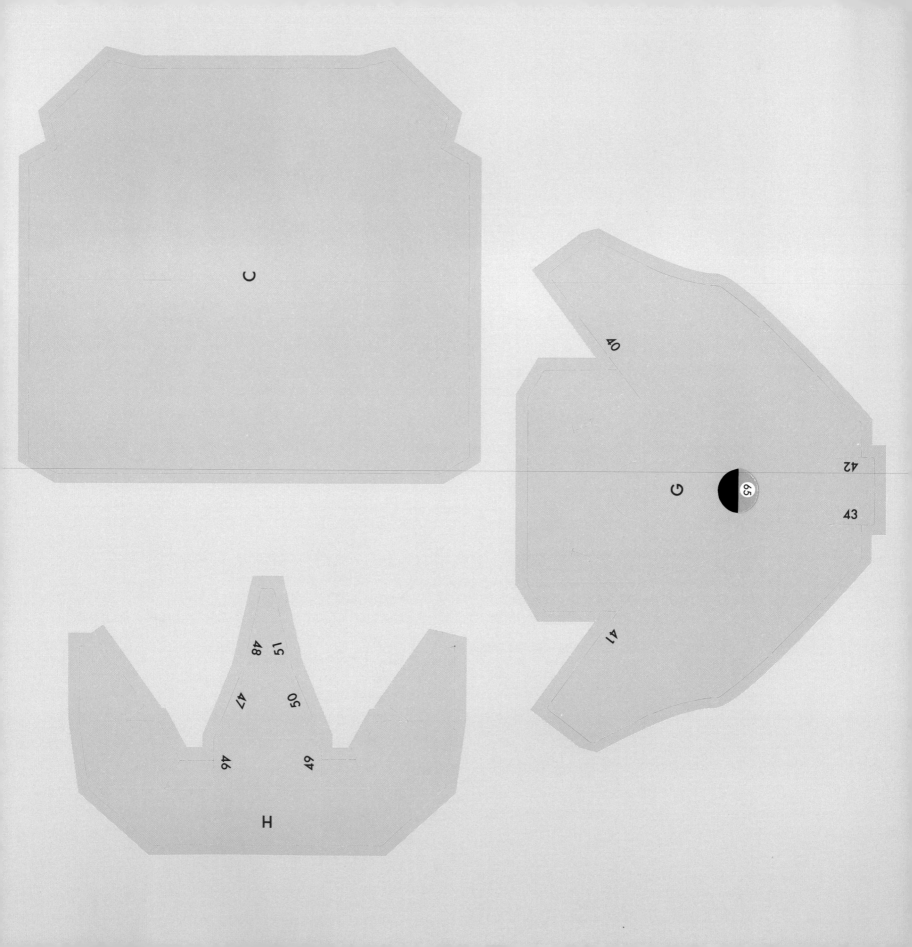

Stylish Succulent

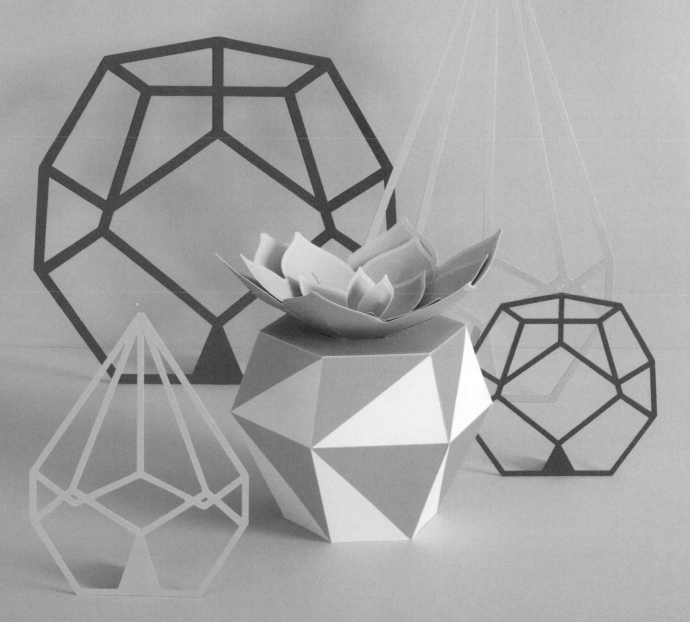

MAKE A STYLE STATEMENT WITH THIS SUCCULENT

Succulents are the camels of the plant world, storing up water for when the ground gets dry. This marvellous minimalist pot plant will definitely be happiest water-free.

1. Press out parts A to H.

2. Glue part A together using tabs 1 and 2.

3. Glue part B to part A using tabs 3 and 4.

4. Glue part B together using tabs 5 and 6.

5. Glue part B to part A using tabs 7 and 8.

6. Glue part C to part AB using tabs 9.

7. Glue part D together using tabs 10 to 16. Make sure each tab on the inside of the succulent leaves is dry before moving on to the next.

8. Glue part D to part C using tabs 17.

9. Glue part E together using tabs 18 to 24.

10. Glue part E to part C using tabs 25.

11. Glue part F together using tabs 26 to 29.

12. Glue part F to part C using tab 30.

13. Glue part G together using tab 31.

14. Glue part H together using tab 32.

15. Glue parts G and H to part F using tabs 33 and 34.

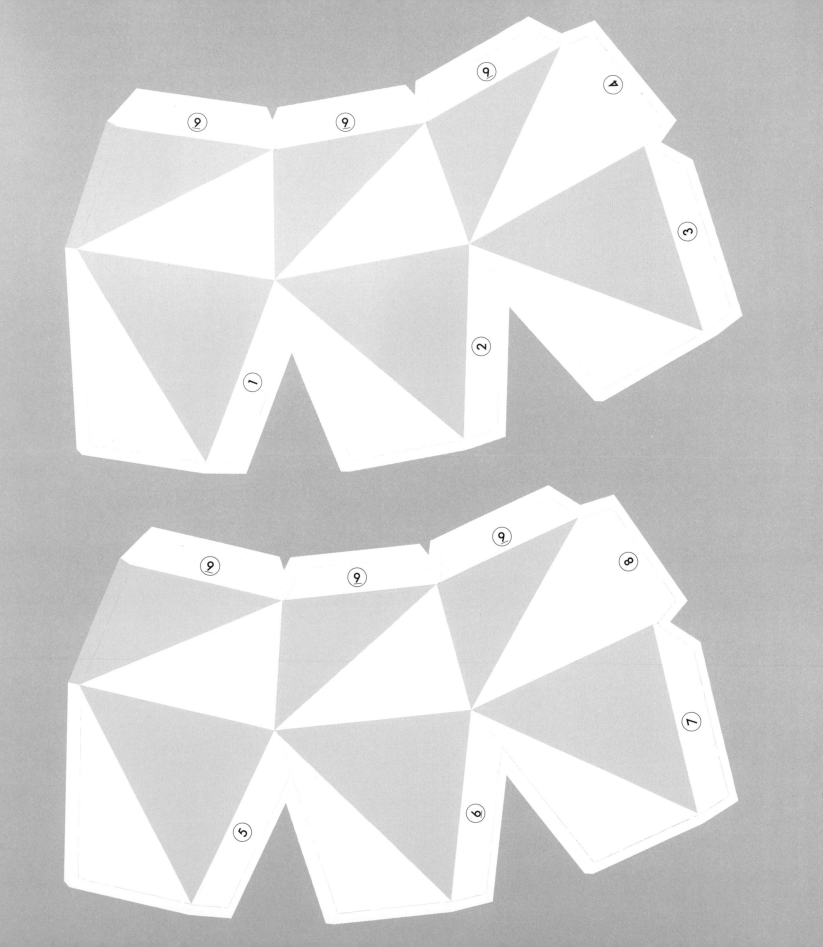

Big Apple Doughnut

GET SUPER-CHARGED WITH THIS SWEET TREAT

Talk about a sugar rush — a giant, record-breaking doughnut was made in New York in 1993, weighing in at 1.7 tonnes and 16 feet wide.

1. Press out parts A to I.

2. Glue part A together using tabs 1 and 2.

3. Glue parts A and B together using tabs 3 to 11.

4. Glue part C to part B using tabs 12 to 20.

5. Glue part D to part C using tabs 21 to 29.

6. Glue part E to part D using tabs 30 to 38.

7. Glue part F to part E using tabs 39 to 47.

8. Glue part G to part F using tabs 48 to 56.

9. Glue part H to part G using tabs 57 to 65.

10. Glue part I to part H using tabs 66 to 74.

11. Glue parts A and I together using tabs 75.
    Apply a generous amount of glue to the marked
    glue points and slot together. Hold in place until
    the glue is completely dry.

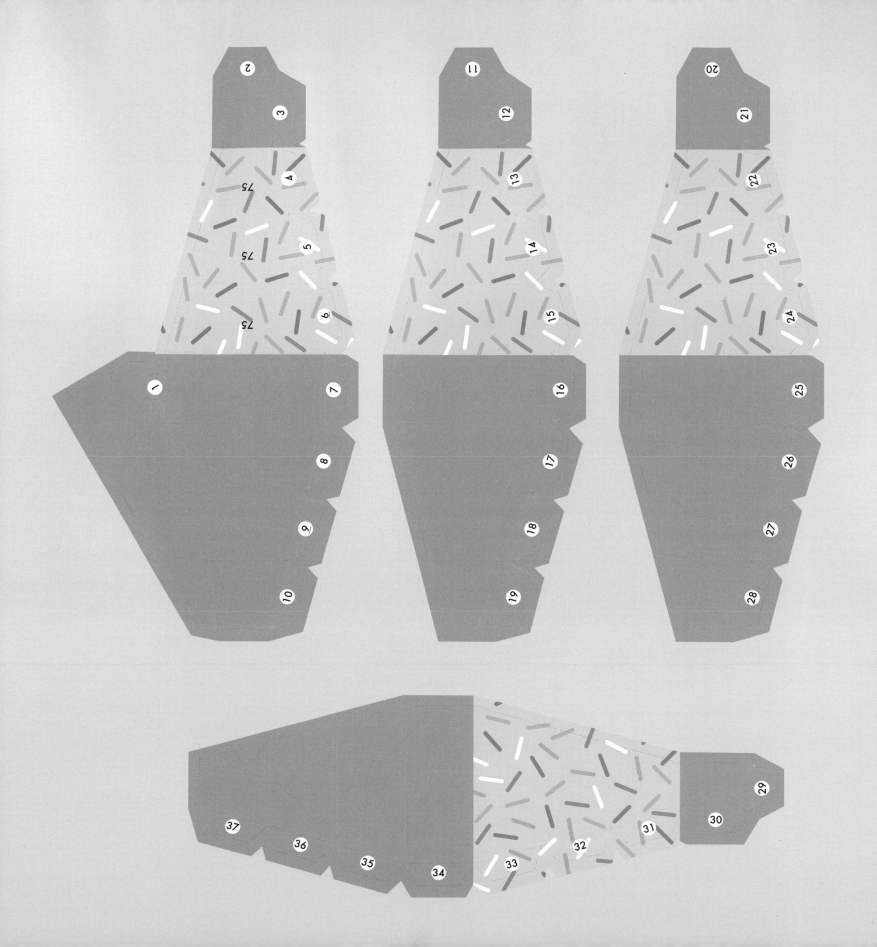

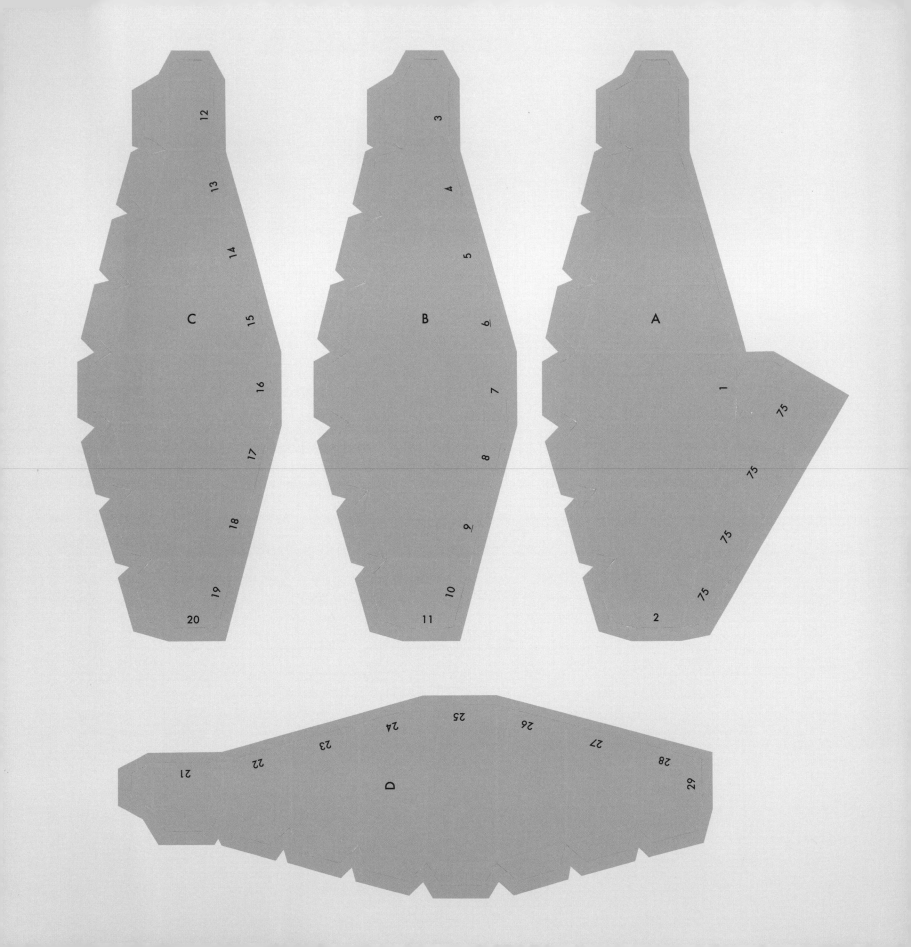

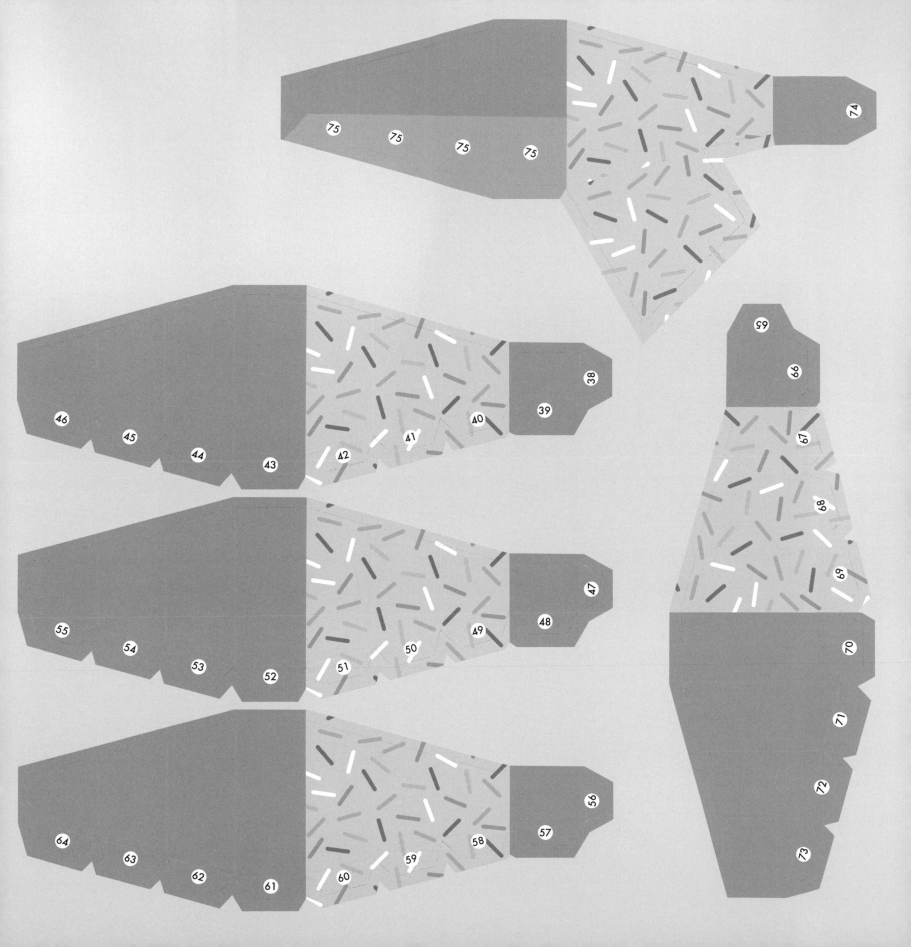

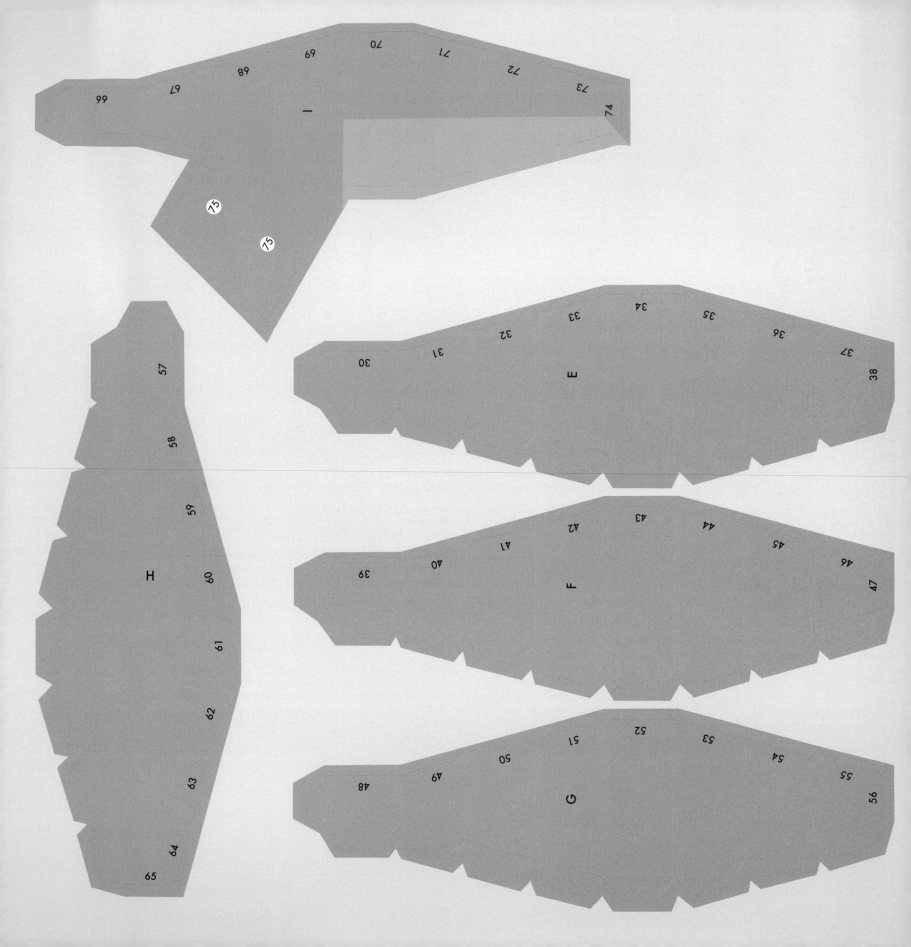

Fruity Fiesta

PARTY ON WITH THESE FABULOUSLY FRUITY CREATIONS

Enjoy the smooth, curvaceous, traditional watermelon wedge while it lasts — farmers have started making square watermelons. They're easier to pile up and store and look pretty cool, too.

1. Press out parts A to D.

2. To make the banana, glue part A together using tabs 1 to 14.

3. Glue part B to part A using tabs 15 to 28.

4. To make the watermelon, glue parts C and D together using tabs 1 to 32. Make sure part C is firmly glued at each tab before moving on to the next.

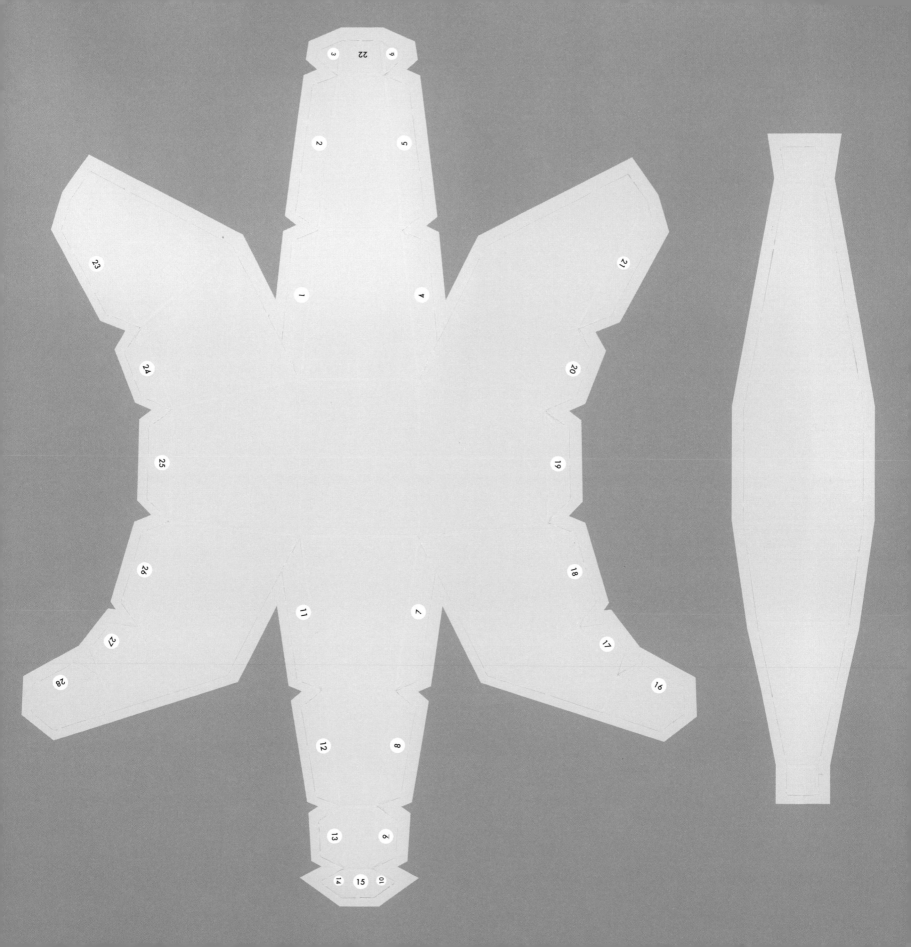

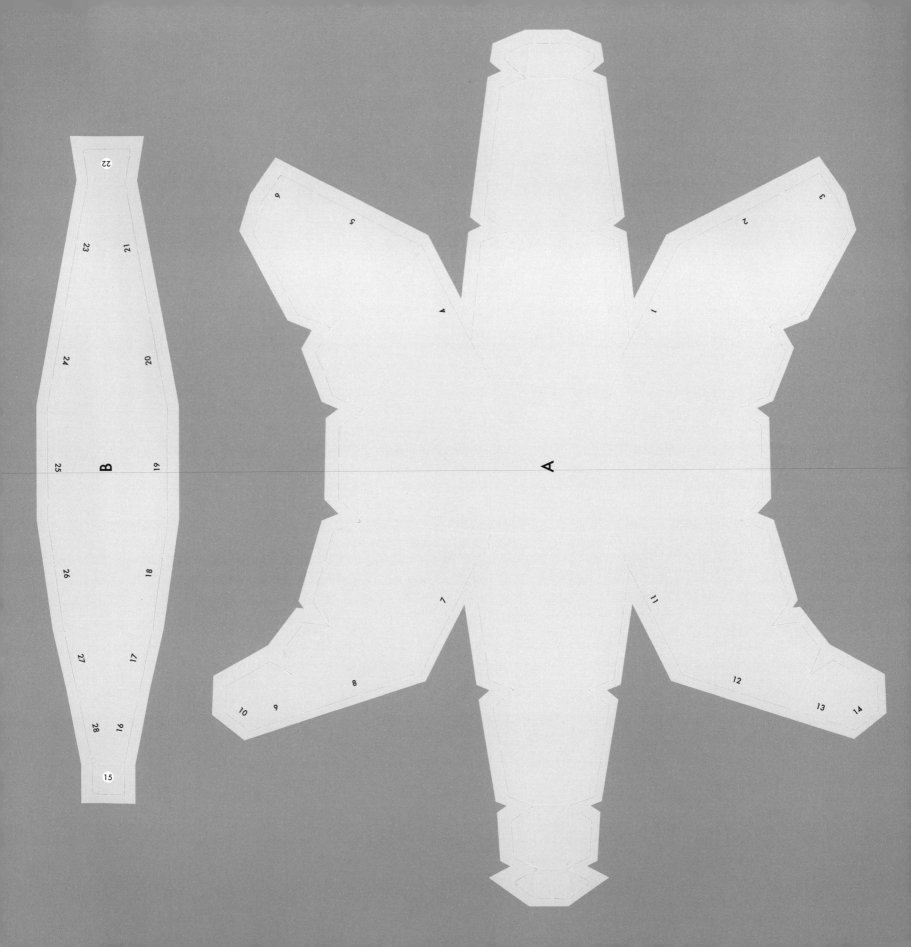

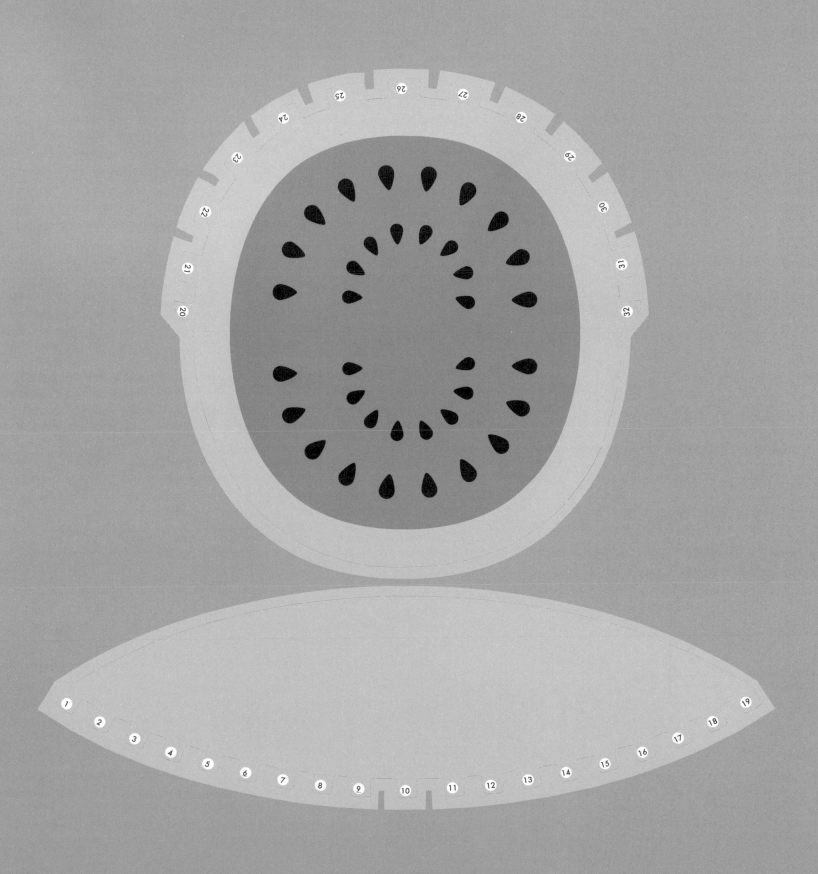

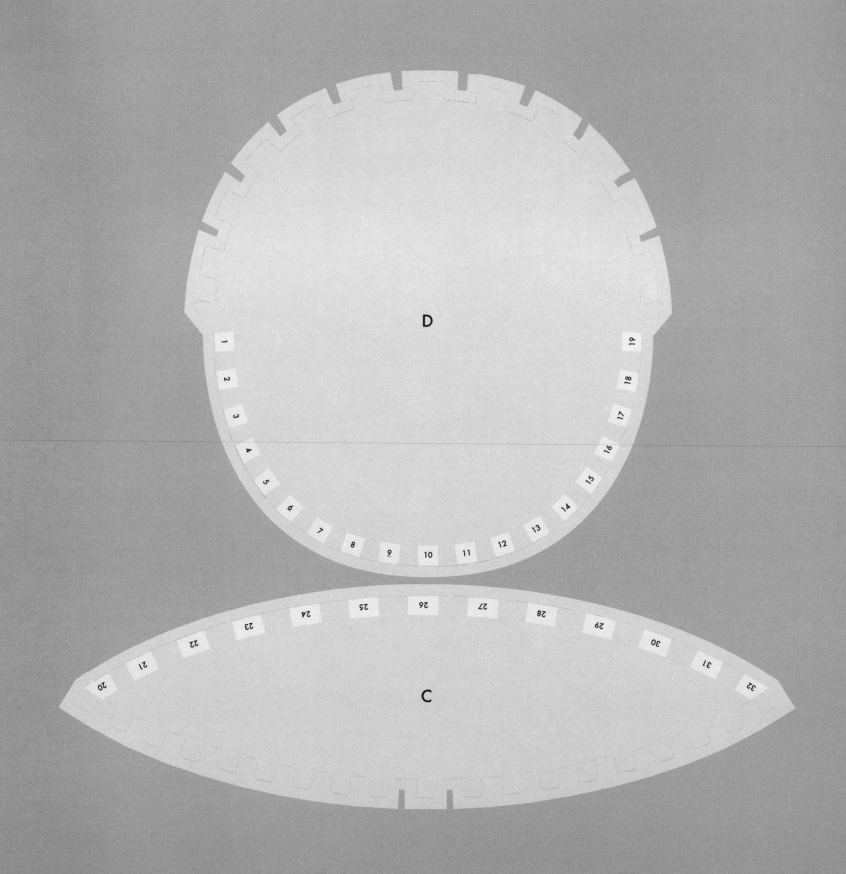

Butterfly Collector

ADMIRE THESE BRIGHT BUTTERFLIES

Did you know that butterflies taste with their feet?
They have taste sensors there to help them
locate food. Better hope this branch is tasty
as well as comfortable.

1. Press out parts A to E.

2. Glue part A together using tabs 1 to 3.

3. Glue part B to part C using tab 4.

4. Glue part BC to part A using tab 5.

5. Glue part D to part E using tab 6.

6. Glue part DE to part A using tab 7.

Party Piñata

JOIN THIS PIÑATA FOR A PARTY IN THE DESERT

Piñatas are a traditional feature of Mexico's annual Cinco de Mayo festival, along with parades, feasts and dancing. Which might explain why this colourful chap loves to party.

1. Press out parts A to D.

2. Glue part A to part B with tabs 1 and 2. Make sure the legs are lined up at the bottom as the glue dries.

3. Glue parts A and B together using tabs 3 to 22. Use something pointy, like a toothpick or a pencil, to glue the tops of the ears.

4. Glue part C to part AB using tabs 23. Getting the centre of the ears is a little fiddly. Use lots of glue on part C and push into the gap between the ears. Put your hand inside the piñata to push the pieces together as the glue dries.

5. Glue part D to part B using tab 24. Curl the tail around your finger to give the piñata a jaunty look.

Snappy Fish

MOUNT THIS CHARACTERFUL PIRANHA IN A FRAME

Piranhas are pretty common in South America and are known for their razor sharp teeth and relentless bite, but don't worry – their fearsome reputation is greatly exaggerated and despite it all they don't find humans particularly tasty.

1. Press out parts A to G.

2. Take part A and glue tabs 1 to 4. To achieve the best finish, slot the tabs through the base and push each edge of the frame flat before gluing tabs 5 at the corners.

3. Glue part B together using tabs 6 to 13. It is important when gluing the body of the piranha to let each tab dry before moving on to the next.

4. Glue part C to part B using tabs 14 to 21, part D to part BC using tabs 22 to 28, part E to part C using tabs 29 and 30, part F to part B using tabs 31 and 32 and part G to part B using tab 33.

5. Attach the body of the piranha to part A by slotting tab 35 on the back of the fish through the slots in part A. Glue the tail using tab 36. Only a small amount of glue will be needed.

6. When the glue is dry, gently pull and pose the tail.

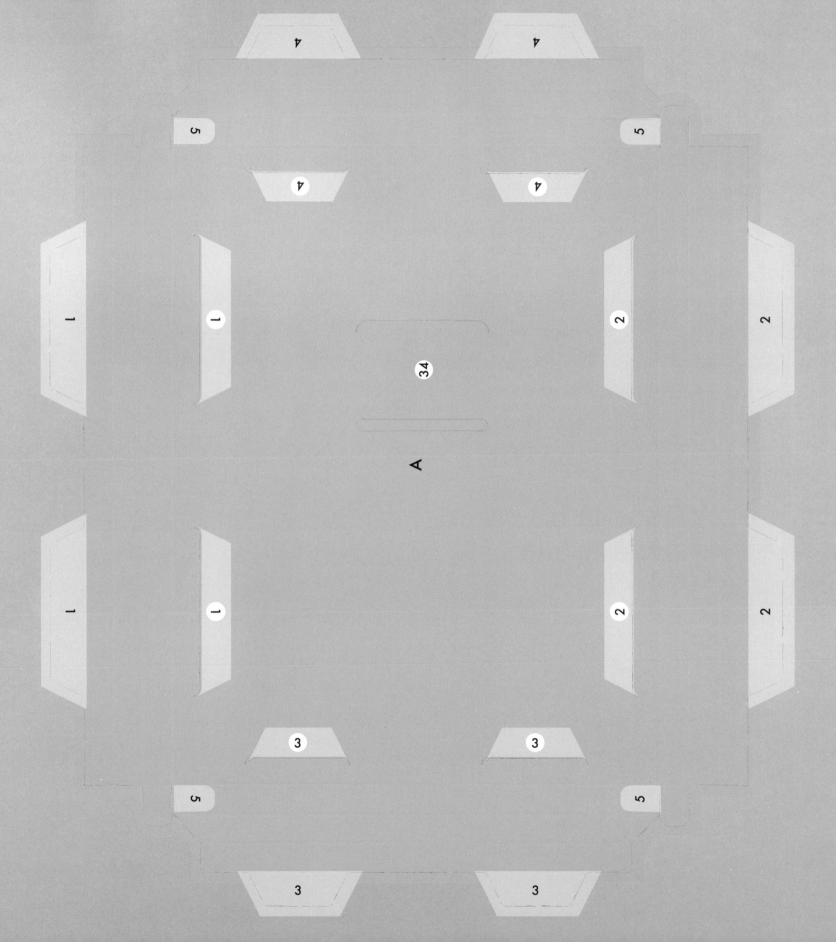

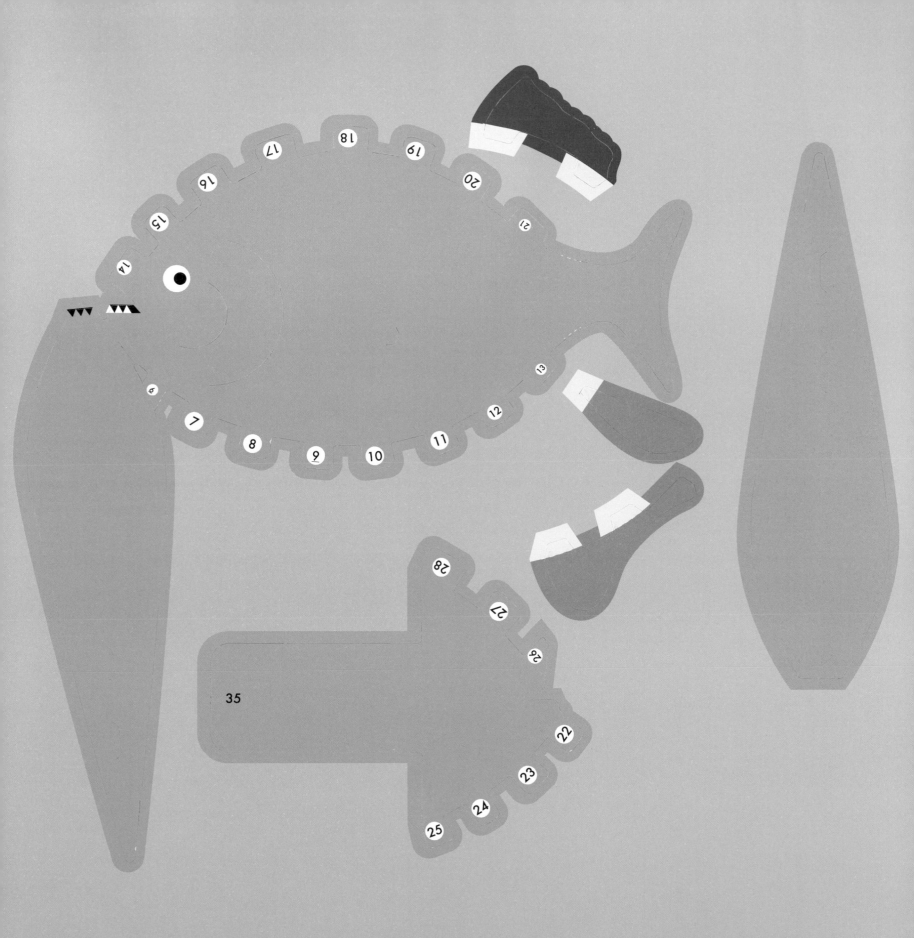

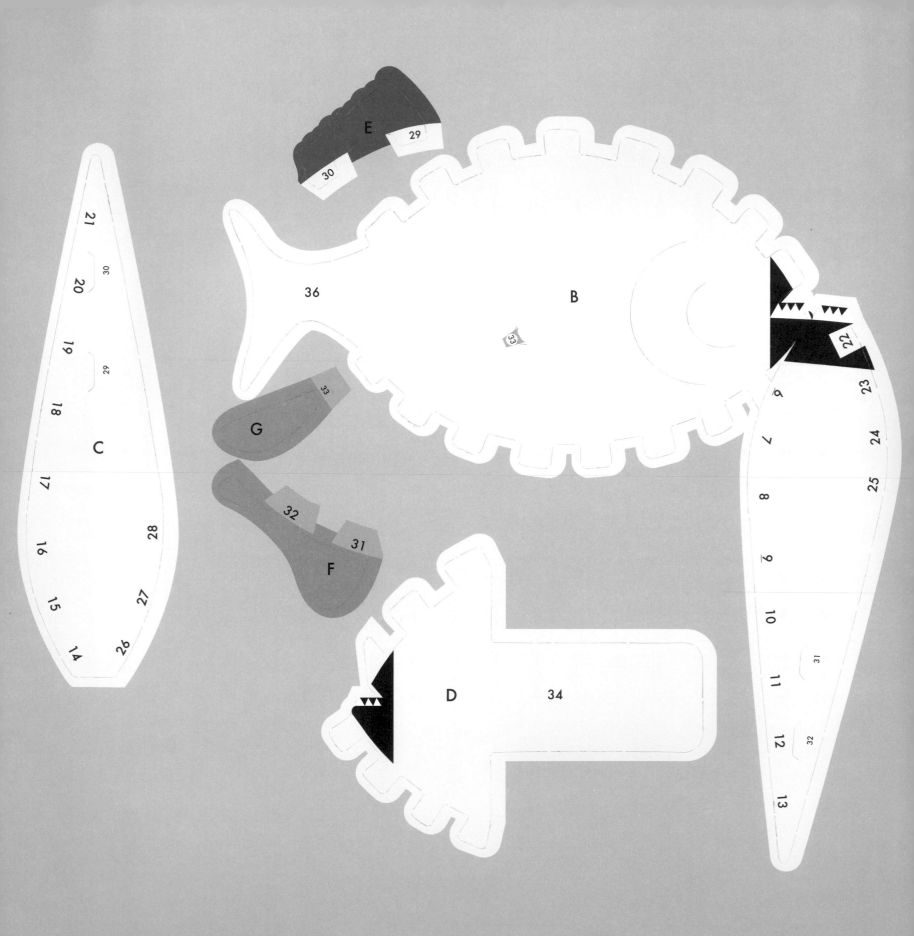

CREATE YOUR PAPER SETS

This collection of stylish backdrops will complement your finished models perfectly. Just cut the pages along the dotted lines and fold in half to create a colourful base and background. Position your model as you like to create scenes from your very own paper world.

"BRIGHTLY COLOURED BACKGROUNDS ARE A GREAT WAY TO CREATE A DISPLAY AND TO SET YOUR MODELS IN CONTEXT. YOU COULD ALSO USE THESE AS INSPIRATION TO CREATE YOUR OWN BACKDROPS."

Helen

Tropical Toucan

Vintage Camera

Fish out of Water

Amazing Armadillo

Stylish Succulent

Big Apple Doughnut

Fruity Fiesta

Butterfly Collector

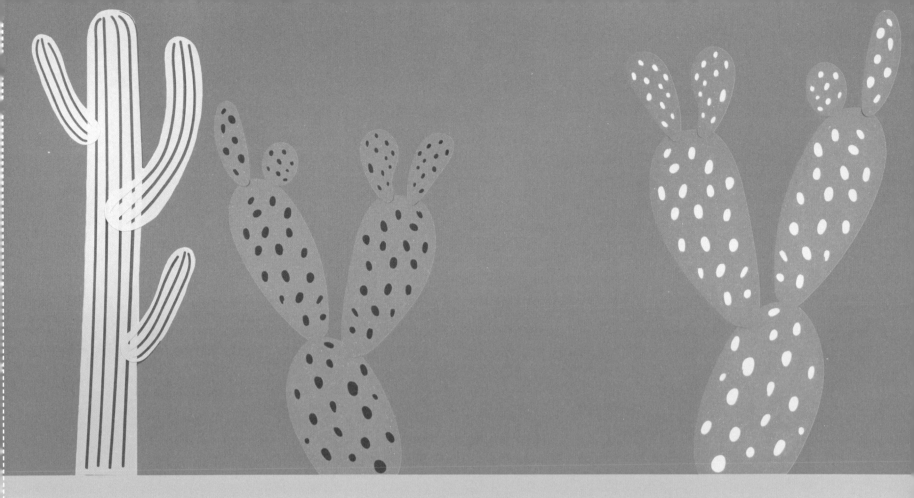

Party Piñata

Snappy Fish

"PAPER IS AN INCREDIBLY VERSATILE MEDIUM AND THE SKILLS YOU'VE USED TO COMPLETE THESE PROJECTS CAN BE USED IN LOTS OF DIFFERENT WAYS. I HOPE YOU'VE ENJOYED THE MAKING PROCESS AND THAT THE MODELS WILL BRIGHTEN UP ANY SPACE YOU CHOOSE TO PUT THEM IN."

Helen